# What's Inside a Hospital?

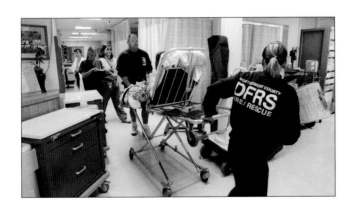

## Sharon Gordon

**BENCHMARK BOOKS**

MARSHALL CAVENDISH
NEW YORK

# Inside a Hospital

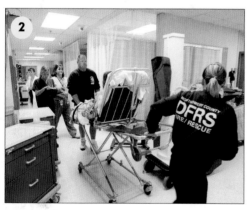

1. admitting
2. emergency room, ER
3. intensive care unit, ICU
4. kitchen

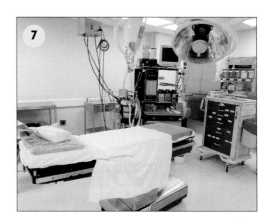

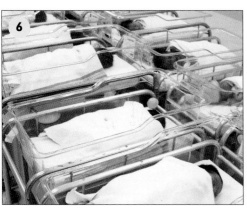

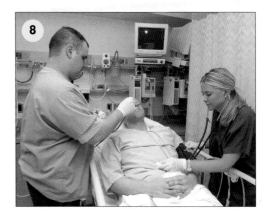

5 lab

6 nursery

7 operating room, OR

8 patient

Have you ever been to the hospital? There is so much going on!

There are many different *units*, or rooms, inside a hospital.

This is *admitting*. It is where patients check in. Someone who is treated at a hospital is called a *patient*.

Hospital workers get information from the patient. They put it into the computer.

The new patient gets a bracelet with his name on it. Now other workers will know who he is.

9

The *emergency room*, or ER, is a very busy place. The ambulance brings in people who are suddenly sick or hurt. The doctors and nurses work together to help them.

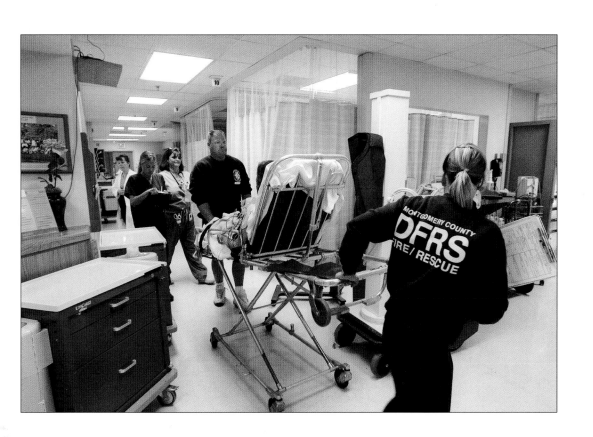

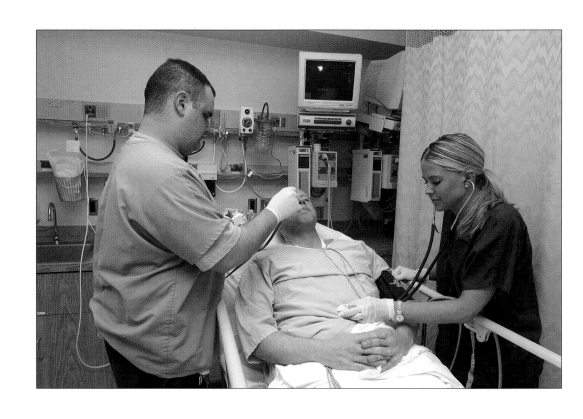

They take blood. They order tests.
They take pictures called X rays.

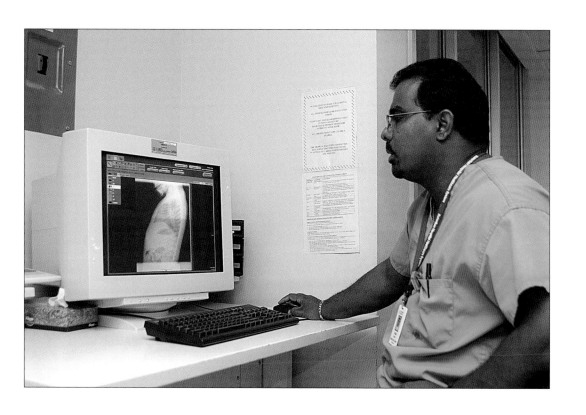

X rays show what is happening
inside the body.

The tests are sent to the *lab*. Workers try to find the problem.

Some patients can get medicine and go home. Others must stay in the hospital.

Some patients may need an operation. They go to the *operating room*, or OR. It is a very clean place.

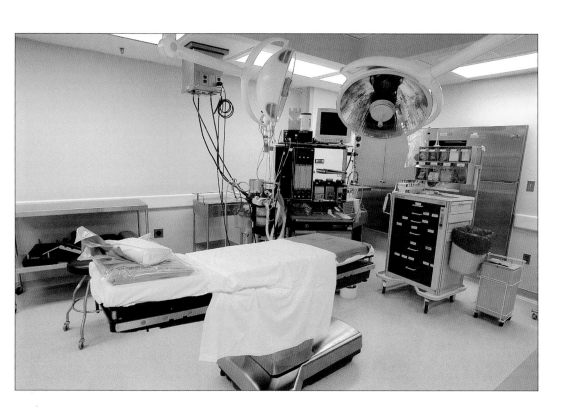

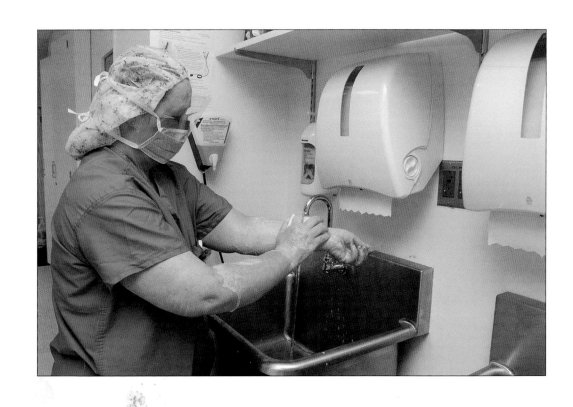

Germs can make the patient sick.
Doctors and nurses scrub their
hands before an operation.

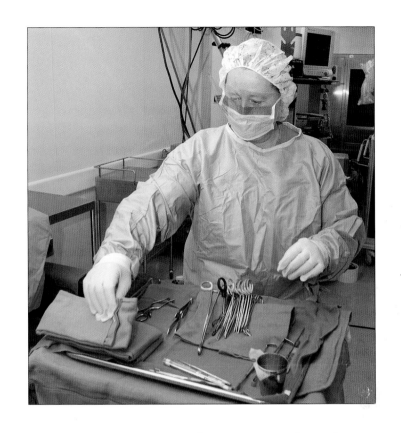

They wear masks and gloves.
Their tools are kept in *sterile*,
or clean, trays.

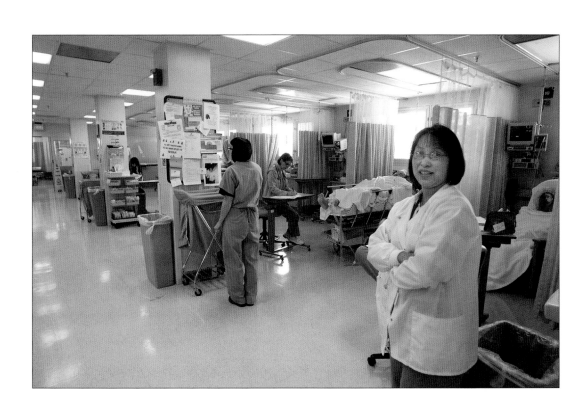

After an operation, patients rest quietly in the *recovery room*.

They may be moved to the ICU, or *intensive care unit*. Patients here are very sick.

Some patients are connected to machines that help them breathe. Others receive special medicine.

Patients who get better will leave the ICU.

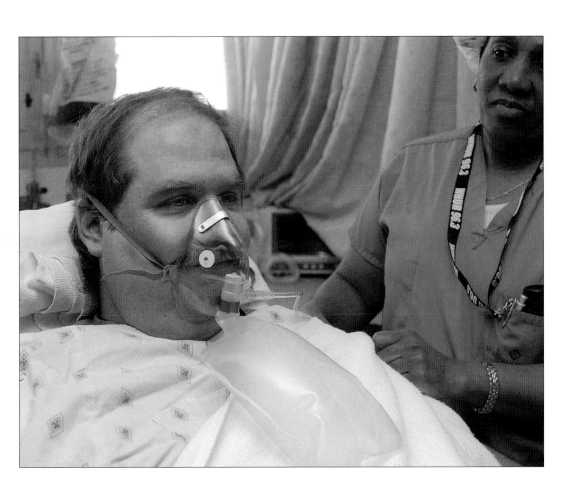

Workers in the kitchen make meals for the patients. They deliver the meals on carts.

Dirty clothing, sheets, and towels go to the laundry room. They are cleaned and folded.

Some rooms inside the hospital are just for children. Special doctors and nurses take care of them. Parents can stay in these rooms overnight.

Even newborn babies stay
in a room inside the hospital.
It is called the *nursery*.

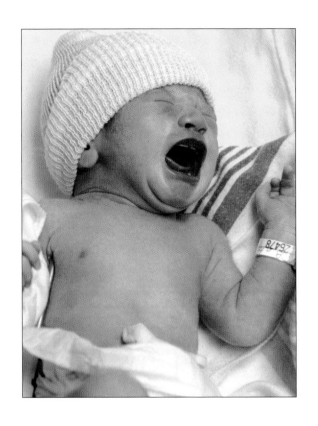

Many rooms inside the hospital are quiet. But the nursery can get very loud!

# Challenge Words

**admitting**—An area of the hospital where patients check in.

**emergency room, ER**—A hospital room where sick and injured people go in an emergency.

**intensive care unit, ICU**—An area of the hospital where very sick patients are treated.

**lab**—Short for laboratory. A place where patients' tests are reviewed.

**operating room, OR**—A hospital room where doctors perform operations.

**nursery**—A hospital room for newborn babies.

**patient (pay-shunt)**—Someone who is treated at a hospital.

**recovery room**—A hospital room where patients rest after an operation.

**sterile (ster-ul)**—Very clean; free of germs.

**unit (yoo-nit)**—A group of rooms in a hospital.

# Index

Page numbers in **boldface** are illustrations.

With thanks to Nanci Vargus, Ed.D.
and Beth Walker Gambro, reading consultants

ACKNOWLEDGMENTS
With thanks to the staff of Suburban Hospital, Bethesda, Maryland

Benchmark Books
Marshall Cavendish
99 White Plains Road
Tarrytown, New York 10591-9001
www.marshallcavendish.com

Library of Congress Cataloging-in-Publication Data

Gordon, Sharon.
What's inside a hospital? / by Sharon Gordon.
p. cm. — (Bookworms: What's inside?)
Includes index.
Summary: An introduction to a busy hospital, including descriptions of
the equipment, the staff, and what happens on a typical day.
ISBN 0-7614-1564-5
1. Hospitals—Juvenile literature. [1. Hospitals.] I. Title
II. Series: Gordon, Sharon. Bookworms. What's inside?

RA963.5.G67 2003
362.1'1—dc21
2003006191

Photo Research by Anne Burns Images

Cover Photo by Jay Mallin

The photographs in this book are used with permission and through the courtesy of:
*Jay Mallin*: pp. 1, 2, 3, (top) (bottom right), 5, 6, 9, 11, 12, 13, 14, 17, 18, 19, 20, 23, 24.
*Corbis*: p. 27 Ken Glaser; pp. 3 (bottom left), 28 E. R. Productions; p. 29 Lester Lefkowitz.

Series design by Becky Terhune

Printed in China
1 3 5 6 4 2